Love Between My Scars

Love Between My Scars

by

Richard L. Taylor, Jr.

Foreword

by Shawn Dove

Richard Taylor has written a book and has a message that we should all stop to read and hear. He is a young man who is demonstrating how the purposes of our lives often come wrapped within our most painful experiences. With his third book, *Love Between My Scars,* Taylor offers a healing salve for so many people suffering with depression and mental health challenges. As Richard reveals between the covers of this book—love is the ultimate elixir for the scourge of pain and trauma consuming so many of us.

Yes, there is no better feeling known to mankind than the feeling of love; not just feeling loved, but being able to show love to others. It is human nature to desire love from those closest to us. And for some of us, we crave that love from whatever sources we can find it, hence the age-old adage, "looking for love in all the wrong places." From the time of birth unto death, one of the driving forces behind how we behave, communicate and our mindset is constituted by the reality we have created for ourselves in our minds. The things we hear and see have a way of seeping into the innermost workings of our minds and where they land can either affirm us or afflict us. As Richard eloquently shares with his readers, the mind becomes the battlefield of our lives loved and sadly of our lives lost.

Statistics show that over sixty percent of adult Americans will be diagnosed with a mental illness or disorder every year and over twenty percent of teens will be diagnosed with a mental disorder within that same year. Astounding, right? Mind you, the key word here is "diagnosed." What about those who never speak up? What about those who cannot afford a trip to the doctor to seek help? What about those who dare not confront the stigma of seeking help for mental health challenges? If these statistics were only for America, what would the numbers be for the rest of the world, if everyone suffering had access to medical care?

Because the mind acts as our reality sponge, we tend to soak up whatever information we are most exposed to. Too many of us are raised in environments where we are only exposed to negativity, lack, struggle and trauma. We have to fight extra hard to grasp glimmers of hope for our lives. Too many children sadly hear their parents call them "dumb" or "worthless" and even how much of a "mistake" they are. For some of us, our first encounter with pain comes from the ones we share a bloodline with. In turn, we internalize what we feel, trying to make sense of it, only to reach a destination of nothingness.

Taylor shares that this feeling of "nothingness" is the urge that drives people to the edge of insanity. This same feeling of nothingness brings so much despair that often makes one feel as if their only sense of relief can only be achieved by death. For my friend Richard, this couldn't be more close to the truth.

Though plagued by the implications of not being "enough" for over ten years, Richard tackled the mental illness of depression head on. Though he lost many battles, at the end of the day, it is safe to say, Richard is winning the war. Not only does he candidly share his past struggle with hundreds of people on a daily basis, but as he does so, he imparts into his listeners a source of inspiration and hope. The thing that stuns me the most about him is that his zeal for reaching those who feel as if they have no voice increases with every day he is blessed to tell his story.

As you read *Love Between My Scars*, allow yourself the freedom to search your own heart and soul to see the parts of yourself that you might be too afraid to show others. Allow your preconceived notions concerning mental illness to be removed and transformed into the realization that so many around are silently suffering. Richard bares his soul to his readers in hopes that someone will discover what it is to love themselves as they are. It is my belief that if one person's life is made better because of this book, then Richard's life has not been in vain. *Love Between My Scars* is one young man's clarion call to the world, that it is time that we pull the covers on the shame of depression and mental health challenges and replace it with a soothing salve of love and understanding.

Shawn Dove, CEO
Campaign for Black Male Achievement
April 2016

x

Dedication

Love Between My Scars is dedicated to everyone who has ever lived with or lived through a lifestyle of pain. When we are partnered with pain as a result of life's traumatic experiences, depression and sometimes thoughts of suicide become the norm. No one struggle is the same. Everyone's personal battle is uniquely fought according to the given circumstances. Some of us have tried to take our own lives, while some of us have tried to extinguish our dreams, but no matter what the struggle has been for us, we can all relate to the fact that fighting through our pain has been one crazy battle though, nonetheless, a battle we can win.

My prayer is that as you journey through this book, you can reflect on all of your pain and the scars that have been left behind as a result. While you reflect, it is my hope that you discover an unconditional love for yourself. You are stronger than your struggle and greater than any mistake you've ever made. You don't deserve to live a life of shame, pity, and defeat but a life of courage, strength, and love. As you read through this book, allow yourself the privilege to grow through this book.

Your brother in battle,
Richard

Table of Contents

A Letter to Depression

Dear Depression,

Looking back on my life, I am amazed the relationship you and I shared for over a decade lasted so long. For so many years I allowed you to take me to a place of no return. So many times I sat on the edge of life and death, searching for a way to release you, only to end up right back with you. I hate to admit it, but you almost accomplished your mission to destroy me. Yet the keyword is ALMOST. And I will tell you this: almost doesn't count.

I cannot understand why so many of us fear you so much that we end up relinquishing the power we have over our own lives and place it in your hands. Do you remember when you first met me? I was only ten. Our relationship was birthed through harsh words from people around me. Every day I dealt with my classmates calling me "fat ass," "dough boy," and the worst of them all, "Richard, the bitchard." Man, that one stuck with me for years. At ten years old, I fed into every negative word spoken to me and about me. I didn't have enough sense to know better.

The day our relationship was consummated is a day I will never forget. I remember coming home that day and going into the kitchen. I walked to the cabinet connected to the sink and opened the drawer. I saw the big cutting knife and thought, *I'm not ready for that one yet*, so I grabbed a butter knife instead. I sneaked into my room trying to hide my hands. That first dig into my skin with that knife did it. It bonded us,

Depression. You led me to believe I could really cut out the fat from my body. I remember being upset because it didn't work. But viewing my blood rising up through my cut skin intrigued me. For a split second, seeing blood and feeling pain made me feel better. For a moment, the pain I felt made perfect sense. Was I crazy? I sure felt like it. What the hell was I thinking? Why did I let you in?

The same year we bonded, I started taking karate classes. I thought I was going to beat you because I learned how to defend myself. All of a sudden, my classmates stopped picking on me. I told you I was going to beat you. I thought I had beaten you. Even though I didn't know your name at the time, I knew we did not belong together.

Do you remember when I grew taller and started playing basketball? With my skills on the court, I had all the pretty girls watching me. I was on a roll because you were no longer in the picture. But then my grades dropped, and my parents pulled me off the basketball team. I remember thinking how I had just lost the starting spot I had worked so hard for. I went home after receiving my report card, calling myself stupid. And then I heard your voice yell, "FAILURE!"

The moment I heard you, goosebumps spread over my body, and my mind slipped into a dark place. You came back just like that, and every ounce of control I had was gone. I gave myself back to you, Depression. I ran back to the kitchen, grabbed a knife, and hid it under my mattress. I claimed it as mine just as you had claimed me as yours.

When I got my first girlfriend, I thought I had beaten you again. I was in eighth grade, and for the first time in a long time, I felt alive. I went to school the next day filled with excitement in anticipation of announcing my girl to all of my friends. No sooner had I made it through the school doors, I was telling everybody my news! I couldn't believe I finally had a girlfriend—a beautiful one at that.

As soon as I saw her, I ran up to her and gave her a big hug. I said, "Hey, baby." She looked at me as if I had two heads and asked me what I was talking about. I laughed and said, "You are too silly! You know we go together." She replied, "No, we don't. I don't like you like that."

A few minutes later, I learned it had been planned. The joke was on me. Man, was my heart crushed. The sting of that joke taunted me for a long time.

Going home that day with you sitting on my shoulder was rough. You reminded me how worthless I was and how I was too ugly to be loved. Once again, I believed you. You were the only feeling of normalcy I had. By the time I made it home, I had my plan of action. For some reason I believed that inflicting physical pain on myself was going to help me feel better. You cosigned my belief. I cut into my skin after school hoping I could ease away my mental pain.

First came the pain, and then flowed the blood. And for a moment, I felt a relief.

You made my freshman year of high school crazy. My team went 0-9 that year, and I couldn't seem to do anything right on the field. I was living in a world of fear and doubt. That was the world you created for me. I remember the voices in my head tormenting me, telling me I would never make it. I could not tune them out, so I played that exact same way every time. From that point on, you became my comfort zone. Whenever someone said anything negative to me or about me, you used their words to help fuel your existence. The more I hurt emotionally, mentally, or physically, the closer we became. I didn't know if I was better with you or worse without you.

I transferred schools, and once again, I believed you had left me. Life seemed much better! Girls finally started liking me and giving me attention. I was discovering who I was without you.

During my sophomore year, I fell in love. As soon as I felt comfortable loving someone and being loved in return, you came back and love left. Your return that time was with a vengeance, and I almost allowed you to kill me. Do you remember the letter you had me write for my parents? Or the bottle of painkillers I had? The only way I could think to end things with you was to end me being me. And though thoughts of death were strong, something inside of me was stronger.

Why did you choose to bother me? What did I ever do to you? You tried to kill me repeatedly from the time I was ten all the way through my college years. I can't help but wonder how many others you terrorized at a young age. When I look at countless stories of innocent souls fighting to beat you, I almost feel hopeless for them.

Depression, I hate you. I need you to understand I don't have any more power or control to give you. You tried me. You tested me.

You annoyed me. You may have held me up, but as you can see, you did not stop me. You no longer own me nor do you own people who fight with you to go away on a daily basis.

While you've intentionally caused me pain and left me drowning in my misery, I've discovered there is a reason why I'm here and you're not. All the while you taunted me, you made way for me to push myself to feeling a greater love for me and others. Love brought me to that point in my life, and that same love helped me walk in my purpose despite the pain.

That love is stronger than you, Depression. That love beat you, and that love is between my scars.

Chapter 1:

That's White People Shit

When I tell my story to audiences across the United States, one of the first questions I always get hit with is: "Did you ever talk to anyone about your depression while you were suffering?" My response is always "no."

It seems as if people want me to have solutions to the things I failed to master back then. People always want to know why I didn't seek help. "Maybe you could have been helped," they say. Maybe I would have received the help I needed had I simply asked for it. Truthfully, that's one thing I will never know.

The one thing that I am certain about is that in growing up as a young black man, depression and suicide were rarely mentioned. The only times I recall hearing about these things were during school or church presentations. Because depression and suicide were viewed as "taboo" in Black culture, the subject often became a joke of many conversations. During those times, I would sit back and study people's actions and responses toward the subjects. I noticed that beneath the jokes, the majority of people were serious when stating how they truly felt. They would say the same thing or something very similar, which was that depression and suicide were some "white people shit." There I was, a black man dealing with "white people shit."

The craziest ideas were spoken about the topic. People really believed they had a valid point in being able to justify why black people didn't suffer from depression and sure didn't think about suicide. Whether it is the fact that we are too strong as a people or the fact that they believed it wasn't in our DNA, I would instantly shut down and try my best not to allow my true feelings to show.

I tried so hard to fit in with those around me. I would laugh and talk about people dealing with depression and suicide as if I was beyond catching the "white people's" crap. Hiding my feelings became second nature to me, and I used it to mask the fact I dealt with both.

I remember thinking I would not allow anyone to try to tear me down because of what I was going through. My main concern was to fit in and never be considered the weak one. I dreaded being an outcast, which was actually a real thing in my community of family and friends. According to my people, "Any black person who deals with depression and suicide is weak." To me, that's like saying he or she is unfit to be black.

The church never fully addressed it and simply encouraged people to "pray about it." While I do believe prayer and faith work, they only work when we align them with whatever it is we pray for. So while praying was half the equation, my question was: Who could I run to? Who could I be honest with concerning my day-to-day battle with depression and constant suicide attempts?

I felt helpless. As a child dealing with this, I always thought that the moment I opened up about it, I would be thrown to the wolves and cast out by my own people. Those same thoughts led me to a place of intense anger and self-hatred. I was mad for feeling the way I did. Why was I given this curse of depression? Did I do something to deserve it?

I was plagued by the constant torment of my own reality, and I really didn't know how to respond or even what to do with myself to try to make it better. I was ashamed because I didn't understand, and I was too afraid to ask someone to help me make sense of it.

I carried the burden of my truth for so long I thought my silent battle was a huge part of who I was. I was so afraid of the labeling and the potential bullying that would come if I ever decided to open my mouth. Because I was constantly told this was a battle that only spoiled white kids faced, I got really upset for being born into the wrong family. *I should have been born white*, I thought.

I felt I wasn't good enough to stay where I was with these "white" issues. The idea of having to be a particular race in order to qualify for a pass to be depressed tormented me to my core. What made it worse was being constantly told I sounded "white" when I spoke in school. Classmates and kids at the park—even my own cousins—joked about how "white" I sounded. I remember being in school and the popular kids would tell me not to raise my hand to comment on black people stuff because I didn't know "the struggle." My young mind fed into all these things, and I really believed I didn't have an opinion. I couldn't relate because I was dealing with that "white people shit."

As a young black man in a school full of black students with black teachers who kept telling us how beautiful our black skin was and that our black minds would take us places we could never have imagined, I felt low. I felt disconnected because I was trapped eating lies people fed me. I was mad for not being a better black man and for feeling as "weak-minded" as my father had said I was. I became crippled in my mind. I wanted to be labeled like everyone else: normal and black.

As I have grown older and taken time to dissect the situations that have occurred in my life, I understand my struggle with depression and suicide stemmed from a lack of self-love. While I performed research studies on self-hate, I learned more about self-love. I discovered depression is a universal human struggle. This is not a battle assigned to one particular race. When I take my work around the world, I see people of all colors, backgrounds, and beliefs dealing with the same issues. This tells me there is a serious lack of education on self-awareness and self-love, not just in "white" communities but in society as a whole.

My purpose in life is to reach people of all cultures, creeds, and colors. With that being said, if there is one thing that connects us, it's the fact that we are all human and we all have human emotions we must respond to. The conversation of mental health is important for all of us. Why? Because we all fall under the umbrella of "us." The battle of depression, self-worth, and suicide is not something that is not a centralized battle; it's more like a world war.

Let me make one thing clear: I don't want you discouraged in your struggle thinking that you are different or that you don't belong. While you go through this book, I urge you to remove the color barrier that keeps things separate. Take a universal and holistic approach in your thinking and allow the words in this book to help you see a different perspective. Your struggle may not be identical to mine, but I am sure you will be able to connect my experiences to your own.

I also want you to know there are help, hope, and healing for you. I can't promise you an easy journey; however, I can promise you the journey to being free is worth your time and efforts.

Chapter 2:

Image Issues

Since the beginning of time, the image of mankind has always been a big deal. From hieroglyphics in Egypt to the early stages of photography, people perceive to know all about someone based on how they look. Just from the way you look, someone decides how much money they think you have, if you're qualified for the promotion, or if you're worthy enough to sit at the "cool kids'" table.

There is a code concerning how we as people are supposed to act, speak, and present ourselves in order to be socially accepted into society. As a result of honoring this code, we have unknowingly placed ourselves into the categories we believe we should be in. Some categories we fit into easily and some we force our way into. Now more than ever, it seems as though society's image and the urgency to uphold that image have been the guiding light for so many.

Recently, there have been major attempts to change the status quo around image: what it is and what it should be. We see various campaigns launched in attempt to "clap back" against those who try to predicate what the "perfect" image for others should be. These campaigns push the concepts of self-love and embracing uniqueness. Commercials and advertisements now highlight people of all colors, shapes, and sizes, but most of these highlights tailor to women. Image issues are not exclusive to the female gender alone; they affect men, too.

I have heard many men say how hard it is to discuss those issues with others because as men, image is more of a "woman's thing." Personally, my image has always been one of my largest stumbling blocks. Growing up, I didn't look athletic. While many of my peers were more lean, fast, and athletic, I was the fat, chubby kid. When it came time for kids to select teams for football and basketball, I was often overlooked because I didn't fit the mold of my peers.

When I was transferred into public school for the first time, my eyes opened. I was introduced to the depths of cruelness children have the propensity to possess. Yes, children are innocent, but I believe you can tell a lot about how a child is being influenced by the way he or she treats others.

Before the move, others rarely had problems with me. I grew up sheltered, and name-calling and bullying were truly foreign concepts. Up to that point, I didn't know anything about the "dozens" or "roasting sessions." In the beginning, I could hold my own while we all joked with each other, but as time progressed, I noticed a shift in the "playful" dynamic.

I was often the target of cruelty in many situations. The popular kids and the "jocks" of the school would go out of their way to make life a living hell for those of us who didn't live up to their standards. On a regular basis, I went through the school day being told I had "titties." (If you don't know what "titties" are, they are man breasts.) Classmates also referred to me as "doughboy," which was the worst. I remember thinking: *Seriously, I can't even be addressed by my real name anymore*? The torment didn't stop there; next came the bullying.

One day when I was readying to leave the restroom, a group of popular guys swarmed toward me. The next thing I knew, I was in the middle of a bullring. For those of you who might not be familiar with the bullring, this is an activity used by football teams in practice. The traditional bullring is when players circle around one of their teammates to charge on them. The goal is for there to be an increase in awareness and response in the actions of the person in the middle; however, this was not the case for me.

While I was trapped in the bathroom, those guys inflicted hell upon me. I took a random punch to the back of my head and another one from a different side. I suffered a punch to my kidneys. Right after that, hands rummaged my pockets in search of my hieroglyphic Pokémon cards. By that time, I was on my knees looking up at the faces surrounding me, asking them why they were doing that to me. The ringleader, sporting a crooked smile, stood over me and said, "Because you're fat and weak, and people like you can't defend themselves, that's why."

I rode the school bus home with my eyes full of tears. I could not control my emotions. All I felt was the constant blows to my body.

Everything that happened that day tormented me for a while. That was also the day I decided to make a change.

I was so wrapped up in what everybody said about me that my emotions had little to do with how I personally felt but more so about how people made me feel. I was angry about the way they said I looked, how white they said I sounded, and how unaccepted they made me feel.

I walked into my parents' house, dropped my book bag, and walked straight to the back of the house. I went into the kitchen and pulled out my mother's drawer of knives. My idea of change was that in order for me to be accepted by the kids at school, I had to be physically smaller. My exact words were, "Maybe if I was smaller, they would like me more." In my mind, my idea of losing weight meant I needed to cut the fat off my body. I contemplated on how to get the fat gone fast. I hated everything about my physical appearance so much I targeted certain parts of my body with a marker and tried to make incisions in those areas.

Clearly, my idea didn't work at all. The only thing that came from my self-trusted operation was a bloody body. I was desperate to be accepted. My being needed to feel validated. Why is it that I was willing to go to great lengths to please people I barely liked? The more I chased acceptance, the greater my disgust of myself grew. And the greater my disgust grew, the stronger my bond with self-mutilation became. Harming myself soon became a lifestyle.

Now let's pause right here.

There are people all around the world who struggle with issues that focus around image, validation, and acceptance. As people, we often find ourselves going through our day-to-day lives trying to impress others. Some of us work to get the approval of others in attempts to feel better about ourselves. People believe many misconceptions about human nature using "if" and "then" beliefs to guide them. We think if we wear the best clothes, drive the best car, make the most money, or indulge in sexual acts someone will appreciate us in some way. We long for others to see the value in us that we fail to see within ourselves. Many of us cheat ourselves repeatedly for the sake of individuals who cannot add value to our lives. And if we tell the truth, some people were never meant to be in our lives; we just desire to have them present.

More often than not, our outer appearance is a reflection of how we feel on the inside. We allow our character to be tainted for the sake of a laugh, just to get someone else to notice us. We become mean-spirited. We take shortcuts to get the upper hand any way we can, thinking only about ourselves and not the people we affect.

Let's keep it real. Some of us have willingly invited many negative people, actions, and expectations into our hearts. When this happens and we become comfortable with them, we tend to feel like we're better off keeping them around and not putting up a fight.

I know the initial trauma from your first experience of feeling the internal and external inadequacy was painful. I'm sure that having to deal with the obstacles along the way made you feel as if you would never recover. No matter where you find yourself in the process, I am telling you that you were perfect before anyone or anything made you feel like you weren't.

Each and every one of us has a purpose in life greater than mediocrity, greater than death, and greater than living in this constant torment of who you've allowed yourself to believe you are. You are a queen. You are a king. You deserve to love and be loved without changing a thing about yourself. Remember not everyone will like you or accept you for you, regardless of what you do or don't do. It's impossible to please everyone or live up to unreasonable expectations. You don't live to impress anyone. Stop adding on dead weight to your process, and take time to figure out how to love you. As a person who has been down this dark road, I cannot allow you keep holding on to a distorted view of your image.

Say this with me:

I am not worthless, and I am not ugly.
I am not stupid, and I am not unsavable.

Those are a few of the feelings we find ourselves experiencing when it comes to our thoughts concerning our image. It is time to revise how we think. Make a decision to release the negative feelings you have and replace them with positive truths about you. Reprogramming your mind to see you for who you truly are isn't all that easy, but in the end, it's very much worth it.

Chapter 3:

Losing My Innocence

By the end of my sixth grade, I had dealt with so much that I found myself sad and cutting on a regular basis. I had lost all control of my emotions. There were times I would think about how far I could take those moments of mutilation. I tried everything I could to cover up my tracks and never get caught. I'd go the extra mile to please everyone around me while I was dying on the inside.

It has been stated that some of the happiest people in life tend to operate this way. They take care of others, make others laugh, do for others all the while struggling internally and not taking the time to focus on building themselves up. This was how I operated at a young age and into my early adult years.

As I grew out of childhood, I no longer wanted to cut the fat off my body. I had come to the conclusion that I wasn't a surgeon and could not lose weight like that.

I went through life feeling sad for so long and couldn't figure out why. Granted, I was already an emotional person. I always felt down and out no matter what happened around me. I felt I could never be good enough in any area of my life. The pain and frustration of being down gave me headaches. I felt alone and scared.

My fear came from not knowing if anyone would understand me if I did ask for help. I felt trapped in thoughts, uncertain of my next move. Some days I would go home and lock myself in the bathroom. I'd look in the mirror and swipe my dull nails across my face, spewing hurtful words. I hated who stared back at me. I'd beat myself up, asking, *Why can't you be more like the popular kids?* I would punch the walls, punch myself, or bang my head against the wall out of anger. I could not figure out how to stop those feelings.

I believe that in those moments I was losing my innocence. I lacked conviction and didn't care for my well-being. I no longer felt I was mistreating myself. I truly felt I deserved every ounce of pain I inflicted upon my body. I lost hope in life and faith in myself. I did things to myself I didn't deserve, but I was so jaded by my own feelings to realize I deserved better. From cutting to banging my head against the wall, I wanted to feel every ounce of pain I could. I was in constant battle with my thoughts, and more often than not, my thoughts won. The pain that I felt was the reason I couldn't get away from the constant self-mutilation for good. At one point, I remember telling myself it was okay for me to hurt myself as long as I wasn't harming anyone else. I would tell myself that inflicting physical pain on my body would somehow counteract the mental anguish I dealt with. In my warped mind, it made sense.

Be it consciously or unconsciously, we all have inclination to lose ourselves in some kind of way. This book is bigger than highlighting the traditional thoughts of depression and suicide. *Love Between My Scars* is about discovering self-love and extinguishing the thoughts, emotions, and actions that get in the way of us discovering that love. With that being said, think about how we sometimes neglect to treat ourselves in the midst of being unhappy with who we are.

Let's use weight as an example. When we are not happy with our weight, we tend to stress over how much hard work we will have to put in to get the number on the scale to go down. That stress then weighs us down until it takes us right back into indulging in old habits and poor diets. Just like that, we go right back to the place we wanted to escape from.

I've heard people say they are fat because they eat and they eat because they are fat. It's as if we inadvertently throw ourselves into a never-ending cycle of digression, and we don't even recognize it. Breaking bonds with some of these issues we face can be hard, but it is necessary and vital to our personal growth. Flirting with destruction only leads to disaster. For over ten years, I remained in that deadly cycle until I chose to be bigger than what I felt like.

Because of my "woe is me" mentality, I allowed seeds to be sown into my life that would take years to dig up. I allowed my self-hatred to become my secret identity. I had opened doors and exposed myself to atrocities that wouldn't show their full strength until later on in my process. I was at the point where I had gotten too comfortable in wearing a mask. That mask made me who I was because I had lost myself in a cycle of lies. I was too afraid to stop living in my fantasy world because I was uncertain of the truth. Sometimes we tell ourselves that living lies feels better than dying with the truth.

Before we go deeper in the next chapter, take some time to reflect on your own life. Be real with yourself about the areas where you've lost yourself. When we are between the dream, we find out things about ourselves we don't like, and we beat ourselves up in efforts to be better.

In your self-reflection, don't beat yourself up when you peel back your layers. I only want you to be real about your shortcomings, so that you may face your life head on, flaws and all. You deserve to live and love your true self, not who you were or who you desire to be but the self you actually are. You deserve to find the innocence you lost and the beauty you once had before the pressures of life snatched them away. Don't allow your fears to keep you in bondage. Set yourself on a path of renewal and restoration.

After reflecting on where you are right now in life, think about whether or not there is a better alternative for you to choose. Ask yourself if you are too far gone to be saved at this point. My sincere belief is that you're not. If you are reading this book, there is hope for you. You may discover a few ugly and hurtful truths about yourself and your role in certain situations, but it's all part of the process.

As we transition into the next chapter, my hope is that you give yourself an honest chance at a better way of life.

Chapter 4:

Wearing the Mask

When we find ourselves in difficult situations, the familiar urge to cover up our mistakes makes itself known. We go through life doing our best to hide our flaws. Some of us tend to overcompensate through our words while some of us do the most in our actions and reactions. Some of us even cling to our professional titles, accomplishments, and duties in effort to make up for what we feel we should possess.

Unfortunately, behaving unseemly not only brings us unwanted attention, it highlights the very issues we work so hard to tuck away.

One of the most widespread methods of self-masking is people living through social media. If you were to log onto Facebook right now, you're guaranteed to see some type of relationship-gone-wrong rant. Do you wonder why? It's because in social media world, you have the ability to be whomever you choose to be. You can say what you want to say and behave however you want to behave. There has been a false sense of reality birthed out of the rise of social media communications. This false sense of being has permeated so much of society that it's hard to tell who is being authentically themselves and who is pretending.

I put on my own mask at a young age. By the time most people started pretending, I was an expert in it. I blamed myself for everything that happened in me and around me. I felt an immense amount of guilt every time I had a flashback on my past, and I overflowed with unexpressed anger. As much as I had a love affair going on with hating myself, I still managed to show parts of myself that others enjoyed seeing.

I was and still am a naturally silly person. I enjoyed making people laugh and liked to be the life of the party when the opportunity presented itself. As things got worse for me internally, I leaned more on my silliness as a place of escape. I didn't realize until later that my playful and relaxed attitude was simply a cover-up for how tense and depressed I actually felt internally. I lacked a true identity, so there were parts of me I had never tapped into.

I didn't realize I was not in a one-mask-wearing relationship. Like many of us, I jumped from one mask to another. By the time I matriculated to high school, wearing a different mask every week was no longer a task: it was a lifestyle. With so many ongoing personal issues, coupled with navigating being a teenager, I felt utterly lost.

Feeling unstable in emotions all the time fueled my anger. I believe the combination of instability and anger is what made me think I needed to become the person I was becoming, and I became an emotional time bomb. I flipped out very easily if things didn't go right. I took everything personally, and I wasn't that same playful silly person anymore.

I had transferred over from a Catholic all-boys school to a co-ed public high school and had made the football team as the quarterback. Moving to a new school was a fresh start. No one knew I was the kid who got bullied throughout grammar school. No one knew about my past, and I took full advantage of creating the "Richard" I wanted to be. I took a step back from being my normal silly self. Once I began being who I wanted to be, I finally felt a small sense of happiness.

Being in a new environment created the task of creating a new mask, and I hid behind the lie that I was a "ladies man." I had never received as much attention from women in my life, and I basked in it. Some days, I even played the arrogant but subtle bully. I talked about everyone who didn't fit what I deemed to be popular or acceptable. I operated as if I had never been in their shoes. Some part of me felt satisfied in causing discomfort to others, and for a moment, I saw how those who had humiliated me felt powerful.

When it came to relationships, I had established a set of standards that a potential girlfriend had to meet. If a girl wasn't light skinned with long hair, her chances of being with me were slim to none. I hid behind the mask of being the "cute jerk jock."

I loved walking up to people and telling them amazing things about me. I had lost all signs of humility and tried my best to become the closest thing to perfection. I walked and talked as if I had no flaws. I remember getting into a relationship with a girl who met all my standards. I found what I believed to be "completion" when I was with her, and things between us got serious very quickly. Our relationship progressed so fast that I lost my virginity to her. Yes, I was a sophomore in high school when I had sex for the first time.

What can I say? I was in love, and nothing anyone could have told me would have changed my mind. I was the most popular athlete at the school, and I had the prettiest girlfriend. For once, I was the man!

I put my all into loving this girl. All of a sudden, my grades slipped and my relationship with my parents suffered, specifically with my father. I behaved out of character just to please my girl. Before I knew it, I had become vulnerable. That relationship was more than my mask; I had allowed it to become my identity.

What I didn't take into account during that love spell was that feelings change, and slowly but surely, hers did. About eight months in, she drifted away from the relationship. I felt empty inside because I had invested so much of my time and effort into being with her. I had idolized her so much that in my mind, I could not breathe without her. During euphoric highs with her, I told her things like that. But those words came to life when everything fell apart. I went from saying I couldn't breathe without her to actually not wanting to breathe without her.

When rumors about us surfaced around the school and embarrassment kicked in, not only had I lost myself, but somehow I lost control of the character I hid behind. Once again, I felt weak, humiliated, and worthless. I thought those feelings were gone, but out of the blue, my emotions spiraled out of control. Back came the feelings of depression and thoughts of wanting to end my life.

I remember the day she told me she didn't want to be with me like it was yesterday. After a lengthy conversation about the state of our relationship, I begged and pleaded for her to stay with me, to no avail. She wanted to be left alone, and at that moment, so did I. Permanently.

I sat in a rocking chair in my parent's room, writing a one-page letter about how I couldn't do life anymore. I apologized for being weak, messed up, and a bad example as my father had once said. At that point, I felt I couldn't be saved.

In my letter, I told my parents I had worn a mask of being a better person but couldn't keep up with my lie. After pouring out my heart on paper, I cut myself, but those wounds were a little deeper than normal. When I felt I wasn't making progress, I tried suffocation. But my execution plan wasn't working as I had hoped.

My mother and father returned not too long after I gave up killing myself. I rushed to rip up the note and tried to hide the evidence on my arm before they noticed.

Failing at ending my life had put me in a place of feeling lost and confused. For the next seven years, I hid my weakness behind a fake, lop-sided smile.

Many times in life we find ourselves wearing masks. Some we intentionally put on and others we fall into and keep on because they give us a sense of security. If you were like me, you would know how convenient it is to jump from one mask to another or to add another layer on the mask you already wear.

Masking issues instead of confronting them causes a ripple effect in multiple areas of our lives. We create such an immense level of responsibility for ourselves in having to keep up the stories, expectations, and lifestyles that keep the mask in perfect shape. But what happens when the mask breaks? What happens when the only sense of security we know leaves us?

The truth is that life is so much better when it's lived in truth. So much extra baggage and unwanted stress come with being a professional liar, so why continue welcoming it into your space? Transitioning from who you pretend to be to who you really are can be hard work, but it's needed and necessary. Your true identity does not have an expiration date, however the mask you hide behind does. The longer you hide, the harder you fall when the mask vanishes. This is one reason why I struggled so heavily throughout high school and college. I let the mask become my permanent makeup.

After so long faking reality, we relinquish authority over our inner being into the hands of chance. Not having control makes it easy to lose grip on the small bit of sanity you feel you have once your mask dematerializes. My goal is not only to encourage you to let the mask go, but to also address the underlying issues that made you feel the mask is needed. It is imperative that you uncover and deal with the uninvited guests that come along with the mask. These "unwanted guests" are those who co-sign your false sense of being. After you've addressed them, you must seek the healing that you need so you may move forward in life without fear.

Because I know what a masked life feels like, I cannot take away from the current and past experiences you encounter that have led you to this point. They are valid, but pausing your life inside of old truths is not the best move. I lied to myself, constantly thinking I was justified in my actions because I was "in my feelings" that particular day.

The only thing worse than wearing a mask is being exposed by others before you have a chance to clean off the residue of wearing it. Do not allow yourself to get to that point. Don't continue to accept whatever comes your way. Constantly running with the dead weight will not only wear you down but will bring you to a standstill. Eventually it all becomes unbearable, and mental, physical, emotional, and spiritual paralysis will kick in and cause you not to function. I don't want this for you, and I hope you wouldn't want this for yourself.

I purposely kept my various masks on to run away from the self-hatred, hurt, and pain I felt over the years. My spiritual and mental pain translated to physical pain. To escape my pain, I tried many times to end my own life.

Your mask might not try and take you out physically, but it can still take out your dreams, goals, and sanity. Continuing to operate in old habits keeps you from walking into your destiny. Make a decision to walk into the newness of being one-hundred percent true to you.

Chapter 5:

Bloodshed

From the ages of fifteen to twenty, my struggle with identity and image was nothing new. I also dealt with the death of my grandfather, issues with my own father, and health issues that stopped my chances of playing football again. I hated my school and the people in it. I couldn't wait to graduate. The growing pains I experienced as I made my way into adulthood were excruciating, to say the least.

I decided that college would be my chance at a fresh start. I would get to escape my past and re-create who I wanted to be. Isn't it funny how we tend to think that we can outsmart our problems by staying in them but functioning in them in a different way? That's exactly what I attempted to do. I kept running from my problems while I was stuck in the muck of the situation as a whole. I thought I was escaping my feelings of self-hate and depression by not acknowledging their presence. While I ran, I didn't realize how much damage was left behind in my wake.

Anytime I would feel any type of disappointment, sharp objects became my place of solstice. Once again, I fed into the lie that cutting myself balanced out my emotions. Finally, I accepted the fact that blood-shedding was never over but was just beginning. I became infatuated with losing blood from my skin because every time I cut, I felt a euphoric release.

My bond with self-mutilation was like an addict's connection to drugs. I was lethal.

By the middle of my freshmen year in college, people on campus knew me as the "Jesus boy." I went to church, sang in the gospel choir, and joined a Christian fraternity. From the outside looking in, I was sold out for Christ.

When I look back on my antics, I wasn't really concerned with having a relationship with God. I used the appearance of the relationship with God as a means to depict how much of a "sound" individual I was. And in doing so, I adorned a new mask. I leaned heavily playing my character because I believed that having Jesus' name attached to it made it all right. How many times do we throw God's name on our mess with the hopes that our true intentions won't be exposed?

As time went on, I started being recognized for involvement on campus. The part of me that longed to be important fed off of this recognition. Attention from people validated my existence and made my cover-up seem authentic.

As if my life could not get any better, I met an amazing girl who put the icing on the cake. Our relationship started with sex and I loved it. Yes, the Jesus freak was getting his freak on. Being on a sexual high validated my existence as a man—or so I thought. My new relationship gave me a feeling that was familiar and foreign at the same time.

Being with this woman bandaged open wounds for quite some time. We were involved in the church together, and that gave me an extra sense of security. From words we spoke in the church to words said in the bedroom, I truly believed I had found lasting love in her. For the first time in my life, I was in a world where everything went as planned. What I didn't realize and what many of us often overlook is that when we have been in a place of lack for so long, we accept the first thing that resembles the abundance we were missing.

The happiness I felt at that point in my life was an imitation of the joy I wanted to feel. There is a difference in being happy and having joy. I gave myself freely to become one with an imitation of love and acceptance. I accepted my lies as truth, and I opened up to everything that life had to offer, be it good or bad. The verbal and physical abuse that came with that new love was my normal. The lies that attached themselves to my leadership positions had me caught up. I was so wrapped up in lies that I never noticed I stood on the edge of a cliff, ready to jump.

Mentally, I checked out. From failing grades to making excuses as to why I didn't perform up to par in my executive positions, I lost grip on my happiness. Keeping up my "holier than thou" façade was almost impossible to do because I cursed like a sailor and sexed like a machine. The pressure of trying to live up to false expectations became too much and I cracked— hard.

I took the bus to Walmart one day and purchased a small box of razors. Six months into college, I started cutting again. Shedding my own blood would become my reality until January of 2008.

The pressure of adulthood took me back to the bathroom bullring from sixth grade. No matter how much I tried to look at it, I could not stop blaming others for driving me back to cutting again. The anguish I felt physically, mentally, and spiritually drove me to a place of utter disgust.

When I looked in the mirror, who I saw made me sick to my stomach. My lust for love and attraction to sex had me taking tons of abuse from the girl I had thought would love me into freedom. I had gained weight and stopped caring about my health. I was too scared to get on a scale and too afraid to walk away from my relationship. Who would want the fat guy? My parents made that very clear over various conversations we had.

The torment of attempting to live life as me was at an all-time high. And in my mind, my life was on the verge of being over.

In November of 2007, my girlfriend and I had our last big blow-up. We fought, and she gave me all that she had. When I say all, I mean every ounce. While she went bat shit crazy on me, I remained silent. I think my silence fueled her anger even more. Honestly, I had no words for her. I was tired of fighting. So I sat there for over thirty minutes while she tore up my room.

Eventually my lack of concern for her outrage made her shift focus from destroying my room to attacking my body. She slapped me, punched me, and even managed to rip my tank top clean off me. I'm not sure if she got tired or maybe felt I wasn't worth the fight anymore, but all of a sudden, she stopped attacking. I saw her eyes shift to one of my favorite Movado watches. She picked up my watch and walked past me. As soon as she made it to my door, she hurled the watch at my face while calling me a "bitch." She missed hitting me by an inch.

After she left, I sat in my room, in tears thinking about what had taken place. Immediately, flashbacks from previous blow-ups bombarded me. I was tired, and I was fed up. In that moment, I was so done with everything that I could not move, which I believe was probably the best thing for me. When my roommate saw the damage and asked what had happened, I barely had words to respond. I muttered something and continued crying with my head buried between my arms.

That incident was my last straw, but I stayed in the relationship because I knew that leaving lead to exposure, and I wasn't ready for that. I blamed myself for what had taken place, and I punished myself because of it. We swept our issues under a hidden rug and tried to get back to a place of love. We kept up the tirade for two months. Sooner than later, our time together was bound to expire. Letting go was not something I planned on doing. I fought to keep the relationship going because I believed I needed our relationship as a means to survive.

I was totally oblivious to the fact that my relationship with her had become an object of idolization. I was willing to fall out with my parents for it, which I did. I was willing to fail in school for it, which I did. I was even willing to sacrifice my own happiness for it, which I did.

If you have read my first book, *Unashamed*, you'd recall me revealing the truth about her concerning infidelity. Of course, I was heartbroken knowing the person I loved and the relationship I had idolized was falling apart. I was even more upset knowing I couldn't do anything about it. After my discovery, things made a quick turn for the worst.

I remember being in her room arguing with her, as usual. The back and forth argument escalated too fast. I was on a roll in reminding her of all the stuff we had been through, and I felt my emotions getting the best of me.

I don't remember exactly how, but I managed to get a knife in my hand to add a more dramatic effect to my rant. In the thick of the conversation, my words manifested in the natural right before my eyes. With anger boiling and despair looming, I got to the point of saying, "If you don't give a fuck about me, then neither do I", and I sliced the knife across my left wrist five fast and furious times.

She jumped back in fear and shock. I stared at my bleeding arm and then back at her. She immediately called for help and ran away from me. I didn't care about the blood I was losing; what mattered most was that I had lost her. I had allowed my very being to be predicated by her. In the slicing of my wrist, my mask cracked and my private bloodshed publically exposed.

The police and paramedics arrived, and I faced the walk of shame. My mess was in the open, and word spread quickly about what I had done. While sitting in the ambulance, a million thoughts ran through my head. But at the very least, all I could ask was, *How did I let this happen?*

I believe we all come to breaking points when we reach the point of desperation. Be it subtle or dramatic, we all react to pressure in different ways. There is always a buildup before a breakup. And I've given you a glimpse into my life to show how one significant occurrence has the capability of changing a person's life forever.

I stress removing masks and dealing with personal issues because I understand the danger of trying to go through life carrying an unbearable burden. Breaking points are reached when disobedience and a lack of personal awareness meet face to face. As you can gather from reading my story, I allowed negative energy to follow me. No, I could not control the actions of those around me, but I could control the way I reacted when they hurt me.

We are human. We hurt and we get hurt. We love and we are loved. You have the capability of deciding who and what you allow into your personal space. It's a matter of making sure that the seeds you allow to be sown into your life's soil are seeds that have the propensity to flourish, not spoil. Growing seeds take time. A seed has to be watered while it pulls up nutrients from the soil around it. Consider yourself a seed. Set yourself up to be rooted in soil that will help you reach your fullest growth potential.

Some of you reading this book are on the verge of a breaking point while others have already hit that breaking point. For those of you who have yet to break, I am here to tell you that it's okay to learn from the mistakes of others and fall back before it's too late. Willingness to stay trapped inside of chaos is a choice, and you have the opportunity to choose better for your life. It's time for you to make your escape and leave where you are behind. It's not too late for you to find and receive the help you need.

Sometimes we think it's going to take a miracle to bounce back from certain things. The truth is that all that's needed is your willingness and obedience. You can avoid bloodshed and the embarrassment of exposure if you refrain from wearing a mask, which hides dark secrets and pain that will eventually come out.

For those of you who have already reached your breaking point, it's still not too late for you either. You, too, are in a great place to make a turnaround despite how deep you've fallen. It's all a matter of perspective and willingness to climb back up and find your true self.

Chapter 6:

True Lies

It took ten years of fighting doubt, anger, confusion, and destruction for me to finally snap. When the doctors stitched up my arm, I was in real physical pain. The cleaning solution they used burned like hell. That was real torture. While I grimaced in pain from the constant impact of the solution running through my open wounds, another doctor came in to examine my arm. As he looked over everything, he kept saying "wow."

With a straight face, the examining doctor told me I could have died from two different levels of impact from the blade to my arm. The first was that I had cut pretty deep on the top of my wrist, and I was close to my major veins. He then stated that the cuts going down my arm were much deeper than the ones on top. He reasoned that it took some time to create the buildup of impact in my cutting. "Mr. Taylor, had you cut this in reverse, you would be dead right now," he said.

When he started to walk out of the room, he turned to me and said, "It's obvious you have a purpose in life, so you need to take time to figure out what it is."

As empowering as that sounded, I was still stuck in my own confusion. I sat in that hospital room trumped in thought. How could I have a purpose? Everything I had experienced up until that point had shown me that my life was worthless. As far as I knew, I was crazy, unlovable, and bound for destruction. What I didn't know was that everything I had associated with my identity and my purpose in life was a lie.

At the hospital, I received a phone call from Quincy, a man who would later become my mentor. We talked about my situation in depth. I was in a vulnerable place at that point because the mask had been snatched off, and I had finally been exposed. I wasn't just exposed to him but to an entire college campus.

It's crazy how the word spread so fast. Fast enough to the point I was ready to drop out before I had even left the hospital. That space of vulnerability took a toll on me. I felt condemnation and guilt. Honestly, had Quincy not called me and allowed me to be in that moment, there is no telling what would have happened to me. God sent this man to help save my life.

While I discussed my feelings of uncertainty, Quincy heard my heart and not just my words.

I'll be honest and say that releasing my demons was not easy. Even as I shared with him, I was afraid of his judgement. I was under the impression I would eventually share too much and scare him off. I expressed situation after situation, mishaps, heartbreaks, and defeats. I attempted to feed him my excuses and justified reasoning for doing what I did. After I laid everything out on the table, Quincy responded, "Man, Rich, all of that is tragic but the feelings that came from them were all lies, Dawg."

In that moment, someone had finally spoken life into me and not my mask. I had nothing to hide behind, and for the first time in my life, I was able to receive what was given to me. Quincy let me know my mistakes were not the end of my life. He poured into me even after seeing how ugly I thought I was. I started to give into the idea that maybe I was at fault for believing lies the entire time. As far back as I could remember, my truth was made up of other people's lies. The consistency of negative things spoken over me and done to me felt right. I never denied them; I simply accepted the scraps fed to me as my five-star meal.

The words spoken by the doctor and Quincy played over and over in my mind for days. I thought if they could see purpose in my mess, maybe I was alive for a reason. I started to wonder what MY truth was. That was something that would take some time to discover, but my interest was piqued enough for me to find out.

Now, I want to shift our focus for a moment. Let's talk about you. I touched on a few points that I'm sure you can relate to. The acceptance of self and the ability to be vulnerable through it all played a vital role in coming to terms with my reality. There will be times where you will find yourself dealing with soul-drenching situations. If you allow yourself the freedom to embrace all aspects of who you are, you, too, will feel better about where you are in life and where you are destined to go.

I'm sure you can pinpoint a time in your life where you allowed a negative seed to be sown— seeds that not only have grown but manifested into something you never thought possible. Some of those seeds we've carried in our minds and our hearts include anger, rage, bad decisions, jealousy, abusiveness, and manipulation. We've gotten to a place where we've accepted them as our truth.

People have a natural inclination to get defensive when placed in unfavorable situations. We don't know how to accept correction without feeling criticized. We get so mad that someone would have the audacity to address certain areas of our lives because in our minds, and out of our mouths, we declare things like "This is me and if you don't like it you can leave." Sound familiar? Maybe not from you, but someone you know?

Perhaps you're thinking about your womanizing friend or mean-hearted boss. No matter who it is or what it is, claiming and accepting the title of "crazy" or justifying a bad attitude is nothing nice.

Living in lies from others or from yourself is a setup for disaster. You don't have to go the road most traveled. Your life has a purpose greater than destruction, mediocrity, or death.

Today I urge you to flip the script and face these lies you embraced as truth instead of covering them up. You are not supposed to stay where you are in life. A lot of times when we are exposed and vulnerable, it is part of our human nature to want to try and bandage an open gash and think that we are fixing the problem. In truth, we haven't fixed a thing. When we finally do muster up the courage and willingness to embrace our process and take on the very things that led us to destruction, we come to a place of realization of times we were wrong. In this place we also get a chance to recall just how falsified we were in our thoughts and in our actions the entire time.

Seeing yourself for who you really are can be ugly and painful. A punch to the gut has nothing on a punch to the inflated ego. The key to making the shift from pain to purpose is owning your past and embracing your present. Do not allow condemnation to set in. Do not feed into the negative emotions that will attempt to resurface as you try to heal. Condemning myself due to my past threatened to destroy my chances of living a brighter future. Please allow yourself space and room to grow.

You can move forward from where you are right now if you change your perspective. It is important you avoid finding a sense of healing that proves to be false. This is a way to fall into a trap that will lead you back to where you came from. Continuing to fall in the same area is not a mistake; it's a choice. It is time for you to find your truth and allow yourself to be reconstructed in that truth.

As you peel back the layers of lies and take off the mask you've been wearing, don't sit in pity or remain passive in your actions. It's time for you to move forward in faith, hope, and love.

Chapter 7:

The Process of Reconstruction

Discovering who you are is an uphill climb. Getting in touch with your essence of being is an eye-opening process. I like to call this "The Process of Reconstruction." Yes, this is also the subtitle of my first book, *Unashamed.* The concept itself is so much deeper than the book title. The process of reconstruction is something that can only come through embracing and accepting your journey.

When I speak before crowds or even when I talk to my tribe of followers on social media, I always end my message with this quote: "You are not losing; you are not failing; you are simply between the dream."

When I wrote my second book and titled it *Between the Dream*, I was at a place in life where I knew I was on the brink of something major happening. Being "between the dream" is the area between your present moment and your promise. Embrace your progress. Once you embrace your progress, you can walk into your promise and purpose in life.

In the spring of 2008, I finally decided to embrace my process. I was tired of spinning my wheels only to be making my way back to the same spot I tried to get away from. Embracing my process meant I had to learn to be comfortable being uncomfortable. I'd have to be okay with being stripped of what was, so I could accept the possibility of what could be. Reconstruction for me was a day-by-day process. Dealing with low self-esteem, depression, and suicide had taken such a toll on me mentally that I had to implement more than goal setting. I quickly realized I would have to fight like hell to gain strength and renew my faith in myself and in God.

Because of where I came from, I had to invest time into myself to stabilize my rapid mood swings. I spent years being imbalanced, so I understood it would take time for me to cultivate a lifestyle that leveled me. I was starting to understand my triggers and the temptations that caused them. I used my knowledge as my tool to make progress. My reconstruction led me to a place of accountability. Having to go back to campus and regain my image while being talked about and judged was not an easy task. In order for me to stay in school, I was mandated to see a psychologist and put on a year-long probationary period. I didn't have room for error in my studies or my conduct. I had to "bite the bullet" and push forward.

Doubt and frustration pursued me hard because of my school's stipulations. I was offended at the fact I had to see a doctor to prove I wasn't crazy. I had to remind myself I couldn't feed into my thoughts so much because I started to resort back to being concerned with other people's perceptions of me. The opinion of people should have been the last thing on my mind. But being constantly watched didn't make it easy.

In order for the reconstruction to take place, I had to be educated and enlightened on how I was set up to function mentally. When I went into the school-mandated counseling sessions, the realization of my own errors became clearer. Having to spend an hour every other day with a shrink talking about my past and present was exhausting. We even discussed my desire to want to win back my ex-girlfriend. The doctor shut that down rather quickly. And

I'm glad he did. I didn't need an enabler in my life, and that's exactly what she was.

By the time I settled back in school, my GPA was a 1.7, and I was in my third semester of academic probation. I felt like a complete idiot as if I wasn't capable of learning. I didn't feel I could be considered a smart individual anymore. I had been on probation for so long that I faced the possibility of dismissal if I didn't bring my GPA above a 2.0 by the end of the semester. As far as academics were concerned, laziness and failure were all I knew. I couldn't picture doing any better than previously because I had fallen so far behind. I wasn't confident in my willingness to fight the uphill battle of achieving passing grades in my classes.

While talking about those concerns with the doctor, he made me aware that I lived in fear. Fear, another seed sown into my life years ago, continued to manifest itself in multiple ways. I had to eradicate the fear of living. I was embarrassed, confused, and somewhat ashamed because I had done some foolish and ugly things. I felt like a problematic person.

I was grateful for the help and words of my doctor during that time because he assured me I wasn't crazy and that I wasn't too far gone. We had discussions on the amount of mess piled in my life. We tried to break down in a year what had been built over the course of ten years. I had to be obedient and let go of issues from the past and be willing to construct the future I wanted to live. Whether it was resentment, unforgiveness, or false expectations, all that mattered was that as I purged myself of those things, I was able to get a better understanding of who I was and who I was destined to be.

Our counseling sessions became more intense as the weeks went on. My doctor was adamant about digging into deeper areas of my life. He said I wasn't crazy but needed to release everything I held on to. Those words meant a lot to me because that was the first time my mistakes made sense. I wasn't referred to as "crazy." As a result, I stopped feeling crazy. It's amazing how words can transform your outlook on life. Not only was my perspective changing, it was being transformed.

Over time, I accepted my existence held value. I accepted I was valuable throughout my entire life but wasn't in the position to know it. Value is not measured by looks or material possessions. I believed I deserved to do more and be more than what I had settled for. I gained the strength not to feed into feelings of inadequacy and depression that often attempted to resurface. The last attempt I made on my life was my wake-up call.

By the spring of 2008, I no longer had a roommate, so I had free reign of my living area, which meant I had more space to focus on me. My doctor mentioned in one our latter sessions that I should try incorporating different forms of affirmation activities into my daily routine.

One idea he gave was to stand in front of a mirror and remember negative things that had been said to me. With every negative thought, I was to speak a positive declaration out loud to counteract the thought. I would do this practice every morning.

Because I wasn't seeing the purpose in talking to myself, I felt a little nutty. The more I stuck with it, I thought about what I was saying and was actually mindful of every word I spoke. Little did I know I was setting myself up for a shift in my thought process. Even though I didn't immediately believe the positive things being said, I noticed a change happening. It's something powerful about being able to speak things about yourself before you actually see the results.

Little by little, I not only believed what I was saying but started to live as if I believed my words. Reconstructing my mind became beneficial to me because once I fully opened my mind and soul to the possibilities of what life had to offer, things shifted in my favor. The mental roadblocks that were once up were disappearing.

I saw myself for who I really was, a smart and caring individual who deserved to be alive and well. I believed in me for the first time in my life.

Pay close attention to my words. I had to "allow" myself to believe, and it took much discipline. I was forced to become disciplined in my thoughts and actions. Listening to myself caused me to develop a drive to see if I could back up what I was saying. I was in competition with me. I really wanted to see if my actions could align with the words coming from my lips. My desire to win against myself pushed me into being disciplined. I had never held a will to be better like this before. Previously, I only wanted to be better than what others thought of me. Shifting my perspective to focusing on what I wanted for me was life-changing.

I enjoyed the space I was in. I could see and feel my life changing for the better, and I was glad about it. As time passed, I stopped allowing the stares and words of people bother me. The opinions of others can only hold you hostage if you allow them to. I was over being locked up in someone else's prison cell. I held the lock and the key to my life, and I vowed never to give up either to another person or situation ever again.

As a part of my routine, I constantly reminded myself that my body is a temple I am not authorized to destroy. I promised myself I would never again take a sharp object to my skin. I had to take time to shut each and every open door that depression built in my life. Furthermore, I had to stop opening doors to things that were no good for my life. I found out that self-worth and discipline feed off each other, and when you incorporate the two, accepting anything less than excellence for your life is no longer an option.

I regained power over my emotions and actions when I realized that I had never lost it. I was simply using it the wrong way. By the end of the spring semester of 2008, I worked so hard in school that I was pulled off academic probation. Through discipline, I earned straight A's and hope was on the horizon. My words rang true. I was capable of making great things happen. My accomplishment pushed me into a new level of thinking. The possibility of a complete life transformation no longer seemed impossible.

The power to change your life has always been in your hands, but it's a matter of paying attention to where your power needs to be utilized. Are you allowing lies to take root in your mind and heart? Or are you guarding the door to your heart because you understand your worth and what you deserve?

Before you continue reading, take a few moments to reflect on the areas of your life that need total reconstruction. Make a list of the areas that need immediate change. Make a second list of all the people, places, and things you've wrongfully allowed to drain your power. Finally, search yourself to seek your life's purpose, accept it, and embrace it.

Don't half step or attempt to cut corners. Take the hard road to self-discovery, so you know you won't pass over anything pertinent to your personal success.

Chapter 8:

Say "No" To Suicide

I can't make my battle overcoming suicide look like a cake walk. Even with being reconstructed in my mind, discovering my self-worth, and learning discipline, I still struggled with thoughts of relapse. With over ten years of struggling with depression, the actions of attempting suicide became a learned behavior. Taking my life seemed to be my only way out. I often questioned if I had given the option of suicide too much power by always running back to it.

Something greater needed to take place in order for me to completely stay away from hurting myself and making attempts to end my life. Physical pain was something I turned to when I got caught in my feelings and allowed my emotions to get the best of me. Over the years, I had become a slave to my emotions, and I fell into the trap thinking that my one problem had to be a life-long issue. I grew to realize and understand that obstacles, objections, and rejections only become life-long issues if I allowed them to be. The urge to harm myself or take my own life was an urge that I had the power to resist. I had to starve myself of the things that once drew me into cultivating suicidal thoughts and actions.

If you read my second book, *Between the Dream*, you may remember a chapter called "Starve the Beast." In that chapter, I talked about how "the beast" isn't some monster or nightmarish ghoul, but it's really the distractions, temptations, and traps that have been set in place to keep us away from our dreams and goals. The idea is that the beast gains power being fed by the individual it's attached to. In my case, suicidal thoughts were my "beast." Every time I acted on what I was thinking, I was "feeding the beast."

As my process of reconstruction flourished, I saw the "beasts" of suicide and depression had gotten so strong because I ran to them every time something wrong happened to me. We don't notice it right away, but after a while of feeding that thing, the hold it has on us becomes stronger. Eventually the beast doesn't need us to feed because we've fed it so much to the point that it has gained a life source of its own. What once needed us to grow is no longer dependent on us to thrive. We unconsciously create habits with these beasts to take over.

For some of us, the beast is a person; for others, it can be a particular place. The beast can come in the form of expectations, thoughts, or actions. Sometimes the beast is our own desire. The desire that isn't beneficial to us and helps us find instant gratification from it is also a beast. No matter the uniqueness of your "beast," it does not need a place in your life.

The process of starving the beast has two steps: acknowledgement and productive action. How did I starve my beast? In order for me to say "no" to suicide, I had to reach a point where I was willing and able to starve my beast. I had to acknowledge I actually owned a beast and then I had to do what I needed to do to starve the life out of my beast. More often than not, immediate action is not the best step. And in this case, it was not. Accepting my reality was the first and best step to take.

Sometimes when we see an obstacle that looks like a problem, we get ready to move in on it. I understand the excitement in wanting to rectify things; however, too many of us move without a plan or a purpose. We move thinking we are going to tear down the problem because we know it by name. Knowing a problem or, in this case, knowing the beast by name is not enough. You have to go the extra mile and learn how your beast survives. Know what wakes it up and know what puts it to sleep. Back then, I could say I dealt with depression and suicide, but I couldn't tell you why, how, or in what ways it functioned in my life that caused me to do the things I did.

When it comes to starving any beast's past, present, or future, you must get to know the truth behind what it is you face. This comes through acknowledging your struggle with the beast. Being able to willingly admit you are facing something closes the door on you possibly trying to operate out of denial. It also brings you to a place of humility, where you can now be real with yourself about taking control of the situation. Before you attempt to gain control over a hard situation, you must first be in control of yourself. Before you try to identify your beast, you must first identify yourself.

The identification piece is so important because it is the key to closing all the gaps between who you are, who you are going to be, and who you pretend to be. Through this part of the process, you get a chance to learn your trigger and desires and positon yourself so you stay focused on your goals.

After acknowledging yourself and your beast, you must initiate productive action into the equation to send the beast into starvation mode. For me, productive action came through willingness to deny familiar temptations and finding the right alternatives. Willingness is the glue that holds the entire process together. If we are not willing to open up our souls to take action and change, the process will be much more cumbersome that it should be. Your will to do better has to come from a place inside of you that genuinely wants to be better and do better.

No one can force willingness on you or give it to you. This is the part you control completely.

The things you allow and deem as necessary for your own personal journey are up to you. I had to find peace with the fact I was at a place where I was more attentive to the hard work I put in than the fact I was getting better. My perception of where I was made me forget just how much progress I was making. Even when things seemed too hard or I questioned whether I could really stick to bettering myself for the long haul, something inside kept me pushing ahead. Those moments of truth shaped me into a positive thinker because I had to learn to give myself credit even in the smallest bit of productivity. Something none of us do enough of is appreciating the small victories in our lives, not realizing this is what leads to long-term success. As I became more aware of small accomplishments, I would tell myself I didn't come that far to start over. I had to keep moving.

Because of my small successes, I began living a lifestyle of willingness. As my will to succeed grew stronger, it gave me a little more power to be strong in my stance for what I would and wouldn't accept. I found it just a bit easier to deny myself the very thing that had plagued me. My circumstances climaxed when presented with new obstacles in getting closer to graduation, even going into the corporate world to work. When I was hit with new situations, I knew my old desires would lead me to places I didn't need to be anymore.

Eventually I became okay with saying "no" to the problem and, more importantly, to myself. When I denied myself, I created distance between me and my thoughts of suicide, which in turn created distance from the attempts themselves. I knew, however, that I would need to deal with my emptiness in those times. I had to find better alternatives in response to life's problems and not resort back to old ways. I was on a journey to find those alternatives and figuring out which ones worked best for me. In doing so, I was able to learn more about my past and present reaction modes.

To be able to think about what I dealt with and remind myself that my feelings were temporary and fixable, was golden. While you might not always be able to change your situation, you can definitely work on changing yourself to become more resilient in those situations. That was how I was able to effectively starve my beast. I still use these same methods to this day and share them pretty frequently with my audiences around the world. Starving the beast takes time, but now that you have an understanding of what it looks like, you can incorporate the different actions in your life to help you become better at it daily.

Saying "no" to suicide has become easier for me because I understand the magnitude of my personal power. Once I got serious in extinguishing that lifestyle and negative mindset, I had a deeper level of clarity about my situation.

That clarity helped me become better in my perception and understanding of what I had been doing to my body.

I believe that each of you reading this book has a purpose in life, and you, too, can say "no" to suicide of all types. You can starve out every beast in your life and walk in freedom. It's all about your willingness and will in application. Remember, it's easy for us to say we know certain things, but it's another to apply what we know.

Ask yourself these questions: What beast have you allowed into your space that you want to get rid of? What things have you struggled with acknowledging? Is there something that you've identified but can't seem to shake? How willing are you in your actions to see a better tomorrow?

Chapter 9:

The Release

Even though things changed positively for me between 2008 and 2011, I still dealt with life's problems. Of course it was normal because, after all, it was my life. While I was never haunted by my past, I was always reminded of it. I decided that dealing with my present problems with the mindset of my past wasn't the way to go. So in times where life seemed to be beating me down, from the stress in class to responsibilities of my duties in campus activities, I really grabbed a hold to finding better alternatives of coping.

One of those alternatives was to find a space of release from all the drama, noise, and worries surrounding me. Learning to "release" did not come easy, but it grew easier with time. Believe it or not, I was forced to let some things go. While in counseling, I had to face a lot of what had happened to me and even the role I played in certain events.

I had a heart full of resentment, and I wasn't afraid to let it be known. I would spend hours deep in thought, recalling situations, words, and action. I still hurt from the things that were said and done to me. I would wonder, *Why would a person be so mean to a child,* or *How could my father have called me his "fuck-up child."* I even thought about how stupid I was to have ended up in my last relationship. The constant flow of unanswered questions often took me to a place of pure frustration.

Many times I walked around mad at the world for what had happened to me. I would sit for hours playing out scenarios in my head, thinking how I would go about telling people off and making them hear the words they spewed on me. I wanted them to hear what I heard and feel what I felt.

I'm sure many of us have been there. We rehearse revenge scenarios over and over in our minds, hoping for the perfect moment to show up where we can use our words like a ton of bricks to hit those we dislike. I tried my best to keep those kinds of thoughts out of my mind, but I knew I needed help to make it last past a few days.

When I told my counselor how I felt, he explained those feelings were normal but not necessary. He said I was human, and as a human, it was normal to have feelings and emotions. He painted the picture clearly for me when he told me that rehearsing the scenarios over and over again was like putting my favorite movie on repeat. All at once, "normal but unnecessary" made perfect sense.

As we dove deeper into conversation, my doctor made me aware of the fact that I allowed resentment and unforgiveness to have spaces in my heart. I realized that resentment accomplishes nothing. Resentment created a scenario in which I drank poison and waited for my enemy to die from what I had ingested. It was time to let my negative feelings go for good. Forgiveness has the power to free me before it frees them. I believed I deserved to be free and so did they.

He also schooled me on methods of releasing my feelings in a productive way. I told him my first reaction to anger was often crying, but crying made me feel weak. He explained that only I held the power to free myself from feeling the way I did. He assured me that crying was not a form of weakness, but of release. We discussed my stigma of believing that crying was for weak men. I learned it takes more courage to cry and be vulnerable than it does to sit back and hold something in that causes discomfort. I left the session that day feeling empowered, and as soon as I arrived home, I cried a wailing cry. For a moment, I could not control my sobs, but as I let myself feel what I needed to feel, I believe a shift in my life took place.

In that crying moment, my past pain lost its power. For five days straight, I woke up to watch the sun rise, and as it rose, I allowed my tears to fall. I thought it was weird, but by the time the weekend came, I felt like a new person. Yes, my eyes were as dry as the Sahara and I'm sure I looked sleepy, but I felt energized for the first time in a long time. That type of release broke down a few hidden walls inside of me. With each falling wall, I welcomed freedom and happiness inside my life. I was able to genuinely smile when I came across people on campus and when I went home to visit.

Eventually, crying became my "go to" form of release whenever I needed to blow off steam. I have other forms of release, like a good old-fashioned "clang and bang" date in the gym or scenic drives while blasting my house music and singing to the top of my lungs. Being able to release those tears does it for me. Crying represented more than just a wet face. My release is not about the tears at all. It's about the emotions I dealt with over the years and finally being able to let them go.

Sometimes in life we a need a good cry—literally, a moment allowing tears to flow and emotions to spill. Many of us go through life carrying dead weight, issues from our past, and problems from our present that, after holding onto for so long, we're like a volcano waiting to explode.

Like so many, I had loads of pain bottled up inside. A buildup of emotions is nothing to play with. I believe it was only natural that I felt the need to release, and my release freed me from my destructive ways. When I look back on it now, I realize had I continued to allow my emotions to have power over me, it could have killed me—well, I could have killed me.

Most of us already practice different forms of release, just not always in the most productive ways. Sometimes we wait until we reach our boiling and breaking points, and then we release our feelings in the midst of a conversation turned argument. I've even seen more than a few people explode and blow a fuse in the middle of their workday on their co-worker or boss.

We see this a lot in the media and, unfortunately, have become numb to it. A report on a mass school shooting here and or a killing spree at the mall over there only pricks our hearts for a moment. When I learn about violence in this manner, I am forced to wonder what kind of built-up frustration the gunman must have felt to take so many lives. I think about the possibility that the situation had a solution that didn't result in death.

Everything that has happened to you actually happened for you. Being subjected to pain placed you on a path to discover your place of joy and peace. Much of the weight you carry now can be alleviated with your obedience to ensuring productive releasing of those built-up emotions on a consistent basis. Truth be told, you are strong enough to deal with the nonsense, and the fact you're reading this right now proves it.

As I work to help others who struggle in life, I am constantly reminded through our interactions that my struggles were really for them and not for me. There are people who look like you, talk like you, and think like you, but they don't believe they can make it like you. This is why your life's story needed to happen the way it did and, more importantly, needs to be told.

You are the key to someone else's freedom, but you can't help unlock someone else's greatness until you first discover your own. You are in the best space right now to find your method of release and to implement it into your daily or weekly routine. My prayer is that through finding your effective release, you can also help someone else do the same.

Chapter 10:

Love Between

As I sit on a plane writing this chapter, I can't help but think back to the powerful speech I gave yesterday. It wasn't really the speech itself that blew me away but the impact and interaction that took place afterward.

Following the speech, while signing books, a pleasant woman walked up to meet me. After I signed her book, she asked me a question not many have asked: "Richard, how are you doing now?"

Her question caught me off guard, so I paused briefly before responding. "I'm learning to flow in love," I answered. She asked what that meant, and I explained I was doing well and that it had been over eight years since I felt down and out. I also told her I allowed peace and joy to guide me to love myself and others.

We chatted back and forth about how depression and suicide are excruciating states of being for so many. I suggested that learning to love one's self in those in-between times is what matters the most. Though easier said than done, seeing the silver lining around a dark cloud is the key to endurance.

One of those "in-between" moments came through my weight journey. During the summer of 2010, I made it a point to get serious about my health. When I entered my last year of college, I was still overweight, and my health was attacked. I told myself there was so much more to me than what met the eye. In saying that, I had to take time to believe what I had said. That shift in perspective led me on a journey to learn about my emotional health.

I started working out consistently, and it was through the process in the gym that I learned to find real love within me. In *Unashamed,* I briefly wrote how I went to the gym and had rough days.

There is one day in particular I will never forget. By the summer of 2010, I had already shed about seventy pounds and was working out with one my best friends, who happened to be a fine-tuned collegiate athlete. He told me he had seen my progress and was proud of me, but it was time to take that progress to the next level. I started training with him, and he did not take it easy on me. He had me doing the same drills he did with our college's football team.

One of my biggest fears was running on the treadmill. I could do all other forms of cardio and be okay, but the treadmill took everything out of me.

One day my new "trainer," Cam, told me we'd be doing sprints on the treadmill. I put up a huge fight with him about how I could do anything else he wanted as long as we stayed away from the treadmill. Even with the fight I put up, Cam knew running would help me cut down on my weight. Because of his understanding of fitness and what would help, we still managed to do the sprints.

When I stepped on the machine, my heart raced. I felt as if I walked into a world of embarrassment, and because of my negative thinking, I experienced anxiety. To my surprise, when the speed of the machine increased, I actually felt okay. Cam looked at me and said, "The warmup is over. Now let's pick up the pace." I had already broken more than a sweat, and it was only the "warmup"?

Since I was running at what I had assumed was my top speed, I got a little winded. Mentally,

I said, *You're tired. You can't go any further. You need to stop.*

I tried to get off the machine or slow the pace, but Cam wasn't having it. In that moment, I felt trapped. My emotions went haywire, and I felt an explosion coming. My body told me I was tired, and my mind told me I was stuck. While I was in mid-run, I burst into tears of frustration. I slammed my hand down as hard as I could on the stop button and said, "I can't go any further."

It was after five o'clock in the afternoon, and the campus rec center was packed with bodies. At that point, I didn't care who saw me while I silently wept in frustration.

Cam looked over at me, put his hand on my back, and said, "Bro, you've come too far, and you can't give up on your life now."

His words stirred something inside me. When I stood, with cheeks soaked from sweat and tears, a thought came into my mind. Cam could have said, "You can't give up on yourself" or "You can't give up on your goals." He could have even said, "You can't give up in fitness." Instead he said, "You can't give up on your life."

WOW!

In that moment, my friend Cam helped me realize my life was attached to the love I had for myself. I couldn't continue to talk about being better without actually doing better.

I went home and decided to write out my life goals. At the bottom of the page, I wrote the question: "Do you love yourself enough to do this and be consistent with it?"

I allowed that to be my guiding light when it came to the concept of love. That night in the gym literally changed the trajectory of my life.

When I started researching what "love" was and what it really meant, I discovered so many things but none greater than the concept that love itself is sacrifice. For me, my sacrifice was learning to let go of what I could not do or who I could not be, and accept what I could do and who I already was.

One day I prayed and asked God to allow me to feel love. My prayer was answered, but not in the way I expected. Love didn't come through magic fairy dust and a euphoric feeling. It came through opportunities to be love to others. Showing love meant coming face-to-face with people from my childhood, my ex, and even my father who, at the time in my mind, was my biggest opposition. I had to sacrifice comfort for the sake of closure. Not being able to respond negatively allowed me to see the beauty of myself through my growth and maturity. There was power in not being petty that made me happy. I loved that I made the sacrifices I needed to help me stay out of troubled waters.

Love came into my life when I recognized that I was limitless in my abilities. Usually being "limitless" focuses on physical abilities or our innate drive for life, but for me, limitless is simply being able to internally become everything I was told or felt that I couldn't be.

My ability to take the limits off my life led me to find the love between. I often read the Scripture 1 Corinthians 13:4-8, which gives me a blueprint to show love to myself and, in turn, give love to others. Honestly, everybody on the face of the earth searches for that love in between.

For those of you who struggle with finding love for yourself, there is still so much hope for you. Self-hatred is what drove me to depression and suicide. I'm a firm believer that evil and good can't rest in the same place productively. With that being said, self-hatred must be extinguished in order for you to find love within yourself and eventually walk in it. Hatred of any kind was never meant to rest in your heart. My story proves it to be true, for when hatred is welcomed in, destruction is inevitable.

I believe that every person who reads this book has a great purpose to live out, and that purpose is greater than destruction or death. The mountains of life may seem too hard to bear at times, but you are so much stronger than your struggle. When you embrace all that you are and all that you desire to be, a deeper sense of power will emerge inside of you.

I stand firm in my belief that love conquers all, even if it takes a while. Be consistent and invest in your best self. If you struggle with suicide from a physical, emotional, cultural, or spiritual angle, understand it is not your purpose in life. You don't have to stay where you are because there is always a way out.

Author's Note

"Love between my scars" means exactly what it says: learning to find that unconditional love for yourself despite your past mishaps. People sometimes ask me if I wish I could take away the scars on my arm and the other marks on my body, and I tell them "no." While my scars might be a physical flaw for some, it tells a greater story for me and for many others. The scars I carry tell my story of hope. Most of us have scars and wounds of all types, and they tell so much about us and what we've had to endure.

I pray that throughout the reading of this book, you have been able to evaluate your life and the things that may have caused you unspeakable pain. I also pray that you understand you are not alone in this battle. People around the world deal with depression, suicide, and self-hate in various forms. No matter what your battle looks like, one thing holds true, and that truth is that you have destiny written all over your soul. You are under attack because you have been chosen to help change and save lives. If you give up or give in to what you feel, think about the countless sea of people who will give up because they never encounter you.

The reason why I love the concept of scars is because the presence of scars tells two stories: the road we could've taken and the one we actually took to help us overcome. Believe that you are alive to tell the latter story. Your life has a value that no person, situation, or expectation can place a price on. Yes, even with all your scars, mistakes, and mess-ups, you are still priceless.

You read it correctly: there is value in your scars. Your value will shine brightly to people your scars are meant to speak to. When people see you living with your scars, it creates an impact that will help them discover their own value and self-worth.

There is so much love between your scars because of you. You are the unique love that so many others need. From this day forward, consider your scars as badges of honor. You received them while in battle. Your scars are not a prison sentence of your past but a gateway to unlock your future.

About the Author

On stage or on the page, Richard's remarkable display of transparency enables him to connect with audiences beyond the surface of the subject matter and continues to be the hallmark of his career.

His inspiring message of hope and perseverance, delivered with undeniable authenticity, has helped to establish him as one of the most influential voices of this generation.

A dynamic speaker, thought-provoking author, and passionate mentor whichever platform he uses, Richard continuously proves himself to be an agent for change and an advocate for life.

Twitter:@trulytaylormade

Instagram: @rltaylorjr

Periscope:rltaylor

Made in the USA
Columbia, SC
26 April 2018